MESUA FERREA

A POTENTIAL PLANT FOR BIOFUEL PRODUCTION

DR. MANJULA DAS

I dedicate this Book to National Institute of Technology Arunachal Pradesh

Contents

Foreword

The author has tried to introduce Mesua Merrea to the world as a potential source of biofuel. Here, an investigative report is presented where the property of the biofuel produecd from Mesua Ferrea is determined and extensively discussed.

Preface

In recent decades, due to rapid industrialization and urbanization around the world, global energy demand has grown steadily. However, this has led to long-term and irreversible environmental damage, leading to global warming and climate change. Global warming has greatly changed the climatic conditions all over the world. One of the main causes of global warming is greenhouse gas emissions. Greenhouse gases are released into the environment through various human activities, such as the burning of fossil fuels, emissions from automobiles and power plants, and bio-methane emissions from agricultural activities. Since its beginning in 1988, the scientific community and politicians have debated this extensively on national and international venues, including the Intergovernmental Panel on Climate Change (IPCC). Concerns about climate change indicate that growing energy demand must meet the need to reduce pollutants and greenhouse gases in an environmentally friendly manner. As a result, alternative and sustainable energy resources are becoming the prime research zone for the reearchersv all over the world. Mesua Ferrea is found to be one of the source of biofuel about which the author has tried to write an investigative report.

Acknowledgements

I am thankful to my PhD guide, Prof. P. Mahanta sir for always guiding me in my reserach and academic field. My sincere thanks to my students and collegues for there continous support and love. Last but not the least I and thankful to the Almighty for everything.

CHAPTER ONE

INTRODUCTION

Background

Energy is the most important aspect to economic and social development to improve quality of life. Majority of the current energy sources in the world are based on fossil fuels, which will someday deplete if we do not develop technologies that could utilize alternative fuels for energy supply. The consumption of energy demand around the world is growing faster than population growth. This increment projection is estimated to increase up to 1.5% in 2030, due to great energy consumption in developing countries, especially in the Asian region. In some related studies, the increasing demand for energy forces the major exporters of fuel energy around the world to find the alternative fuels to replace products based on fossil fuel, and not to be dependent on it. Sustainability is the main issue that causes the energy sector not being fully developed, thus various agencies are required to utilize new and renewable energy sources. Biodiesel is one of the most promising alternative fuels to solve this problem. Biodiesel is renewable, biodegradable, and non-toxic and has almost very close property to that of diesel fuel. It can be produced from vegetable oils, as well as animal fats. These oils, however, have high viscosity and is therefore cannot be directly used as fuel. In order to reduce viscosity, the raw oils must undergo trans-esterification process to remove glycerine as by product and esters, thus creating biodiesel. Biodiesel can operate in compression-ignition engines with little or no modification, similar to petroleum diesel. Moreover, biodiesel has more advantages regarding the engine wear, cost, and availability. When burned, biodiesel produces pollutants that are less detrimental to human health. In addition, it provides better lubricity as compared to diesel fuel. However, performance and emission characteristics of biodiesel-fuelled engine are important to consider. In general, combustion of biodiesel fuel in compression-ignition

(CI) engines produces less smoke, particulate matter, carbon monoxide and hydrocarbon emission. These achievements are influenced by several factors, including lower heating value, increased viscosity, higher density, less calorific value and oxygen content of biodiesel. In order to improve the viscosity, reduce fuel consumption and obtain adverse effect, many researchers had tried adding different blending components such as methanol. Reduction of the NOx emission had also been focused on by modifying the properties of biodiesel itself, adjusting the engine setting and others.

Energy- India and World Scenarios

Energy is needed for economic growth, for improving the quality of life and for increasing opportunities for development. Ensuring life line supply of clean energy to all is essential for nurturing inclusive growth, meeting the millennium development goals and raising India's human development index that compares poorly with several countries that are currently below India's level of development. The broad vision behind India's integrated energy policy is to reliably meet the demand for energy services of all sectors including the transport sector in all parts of the country with safe, clean and convenient energy at the least-cost. This must be done in a technically efficient, economically viable and environmentally sustainable manner using different fuels and forms of energy, conventional and non-conventional. In other words, the goal of the energy policy is to provide energy security to all. Table1 shows that the amount of non-conventional sources of energy is comparatively less. Thus, there is a need of using the renewable sources of energy due to the fast depletion of the fossil fuels. The present world energy scenario has stimulated active research interest in non-petroleum, renewable and non-polluting fuels. The world reserves of primary energy and raw materials are obviously limited. According to an estimate, the reserves will last only another 218 years for coal, 41 years for oil and 63 years for natural gas, under a business- as usual scenario.

Following the record oil prices associated with the Iranian revolution in 1979 to 1980 and with the start of the Iran-Iraq war in 1980, there was a drop in the total world oil consumption, from about 63 million barrel per day in 1980 to 59 million barrel per day in 1983. Since then world consumption of petroleum product has increased, totaling of about 84 million barrels per day in 2005**(GAO-07-283)**. Being the fifth largest energy consumer, India imported nearly 70% of its crude oil requirement during 2003-04. Estimates indicate this figures will rise to 95% by 2030 **(World**

Energy Outlook 2005).Thus, much push is required in the usage of Biodiesel and Biogas in India as well as in the whole world, especially in the transport sector, as large energy consumption occurs in this sector.

ALTERNATE SOURCES OF ENERGY

Why Alternate Sources Of Energy?

Energy sources like crude oil, coal and natural gas are essential for various purposes. Most of our day-to-day activities will come to a standstill if these energy sources are not available to us. There is an ongoing debate whether we require alternative energy sources or if there are enough energy sources like crude oil and natural gas to meet the growing demands of individuals and industries throughout the world. Due to the growing population there will be more demand for energy resources in future. It is believed that fossil fuels such as natural gas and crude oil will get depleted after few decades. Though technology has paved way for oil companies to extract oil from unproved oil reserves there is no guarantee that the future demand for these fossil fuels can be met.

Fossil fuels like natural gas and crude oil are non renewable as well as harmful to the environment upon burning. Hence the need for an alternative energy source arises. Fossil fuels are naturally occurring energy sources, which are formed from dead plants, and creatures buried under soil some millions of years ago. At the current rate of consumption it's difficult to extract newly formed fossil fuels as the rate of production of such fossil fuels is extremely slow which will take hundreds of years. Alternative energy source like solar power is natural and renewable. Fossil fuels contribute largely to global warming which has become a major environmental issue. Solar need of crude oil for transportation, which proves expensive. An alternative energy, which is less expensive and wind energy will not get depleted unlike crude oil and they can be used repeatedly.

People are slowly switching to alternative energy sources due to its varied advantages over the limited stock of non-renewable energy sources. Few countries have already realized the need for using energy sources like wind and solar power. It's not possible for the entire world to be fully dependent upon fossil fuels. Using alternative energy sources will help in saving fossil fuels like crude oil and natural gas for emergency use in future. Investing money in energy sources like solar power will help consumers in the long run. The price of crude oil is skyrocketing and the underdeveloped countries find it difficult to consume such energy sources.

Many countries are in and less harmful to the environment, will be a boon to underdeveloped countries.

Different types of Alternate Fuels:

Liquefied Petroleum Gas (LPG)

Liquefied petroleum gas, as the name suggests, is partly a byproduct of petroleum refining.. It consists of hydrocarbons that are vapors, rather than liquids, at normal temperatures and pressures, but which turn liquid at moderate pressures; its main constituent is propane, and it is sometimes referred to by that name.

Advantages

LPG is safer than gasoline. It is also somewhat cheaper than gasoline in most places at most times, when you compare the price of a gallon of gasoline with the price of the somewhat larger volume of LPG needed to drive the same distance.

Disadvantages

LPG is, again, in some ways the least "alternative" of alternative fuels; because its source is partly petroleum, it does less to help relieve the petroleum dependency problem than some other alternative fuels. It's somewhat lower energy content compared to gasoline means you need a slightly bigger tank to get the same driving range; the tank will also be heavier because it has to be strong enough to withstand the LPG storage pressure.

Compressed Natural Gas (CNG)

Natural gas is the same stuff that heats your stove or your house. It is largely produced domestically; it can be imported through pipelines or as a cryogenic (super-cold) liquid on special tanker ships, but because this is a lot harder than pouring crude or refined oil into a tanker or a pipeline, we haven't built up an import dependency for natural gas as we have for petroleum.

Advantages

Compressed natural gas is like <u>liquefied petroleum gas</u> (LPG) in many ways, only more so. It is very easy on the engine, giving longer service life and lower maintenance costs. CNG is the least expensive alternative fuel (except <u>electricity</u>) when you compare equal amounts of fuel energy.

Disadvantages

Again, CNG is like LPG, but more so. The tanks are quite bulky and heavy, about three times more so than LPG tanks, though modern composite technology is starting to be used to cut weight and cost (as on the Honda Civic GX). And again, mostly because of the heavy-duty tanks, there is currently a large price premium for a CNG vehicle compared to a gasoline version. The fuel and maintenance costs can be enough cheaper, however in a high-mileage application like a transit bus, a taxi, or a shuttle van, that this will repay the higher initial purchase price over time. Finally, the refueling infrastructure is still growing.

Methanol

Methanol is typically made from natural gas; though it is possible to produce it by fermenting biomass (this is why it is sometimes called "wood alcohol"), this is not economically competitive yet. Because it is easier to transport natural gas to a distant market by converting it to methanol, which is a liquid at ordinary temperatures and pressures, than by chilling and liquefying it or by building a long pipeline, some petroleum-exporting countries are looking at exporting their "waste" natural gas by converting it to methanol; however, most of the natural gas that goes into methanol is still domestically produced.

Advantages

Alcohol fuels like M85 are perhaps the most "transparent" alternative fuels to the user, i.e., they are the least distinguishable from gasoline in how you buy and use them, which should ease acceptance. The fuel system of a car or truck only needs to be slightly changed in order for it to run on M85, and recently automakers have been offering M85 vehicles at no extra cost over their gasoline counterparts, though at present automakers seem to be more interested in ethanol (E85).

Disadvantages

Methanol is more corrosive than gasoline (though it is less toxic) .This is why an automaker needs to change some of the materials in the fuel-handling systems of both the vehicle and the refueling station to materials that can withstand attack by the fuel. Special oil additives are necessary in order to protect the engine. Also, because the mixture of air to fuel is much richer than gasoline (about 8 to 1 by weight, compared to about 14 to 1 for gasoline), there is more liquid fuel available to wash oil off of cylinder walls during a cold start.

Ethanol

Ethanol, or grain alcohol, is produced by fermenting biomass, commonly corn (though other, lower-value feed stocks have been tested in an effort to reduce costs, like brewery waste). It is thus inherently a renewable resource, and contributes nothing in itself to greenhouse-gas loading of the atmosphere.

Advantages

Ethanol, as noted above, is a renewable resource that contributes nothing in itself to global warming concerns. Like methanol, it can be blended with any amount of gasoline in the tank of a flex-fuel vehicle, which is what automakers are selling these days. In fact, starting with the 1999 model year, some automakers are making every one of certain vehicle models capable of using E85 in any mixture with gasoline, at no extra charge.

Disadvantages

The main disadvantage of E85 is the price of the fuel, even with the available subsidies. Ethanol is somewhat corrosive, though less so than methanol, and concerns about vapor lock.

Electricity

Electricity can be made by many means, from the burning of high-sulfur coal to pollution-free photovoltaic cells (or solar cells). Electric vehicles are generally divided into battery and hybrid classes, depending on whether the electricity is generated off-board and stored in a battery or generated by a small on-board power plant. Hybrid electric vehicles can be designed to run on any fuel, including gasoline or diesel as well as alternative fuels, and can best be thought of as highly-efficient gasoline, diesel, or alternative-fueled vehicles.

Advantages

Electric vehicles have the potential to be by far the cleanest means of transportation, and even in the near term it takes a very advanced natural-gas-powered vehicle like the Honda Civic GX to give them a run for their money in terms of low pollution.

Disadvantages

The biggest real disadvantage of electric vehicles, at present, is their higher price; even today, though, if you need a vehicle to do a lot of stop-and-go driving and idling, which wastes a lot of fuel and is veryhard on an internal combustion engine, you can save enough in fuel and repairs to make an electric vehicle pay for itself even without the substantial tax credits and other subsidies that are available.

1.3 BIODIESEL

Biodiesel is a liquid biofuel obtained by chemical processes from vegetable oils or animal fats and an alcohol that can be used in diesel engines, alone or blended with diesel oil. ASTM International (originally known as the American Society for Testing and Materials) defines biodiesel as a mixture of long-chain monoalkylic esters from fatty acids obtained from renewable resources, to be used in diesel engines. Blends with diesel fuel are indicated as "Bx", where "x" is the percentage of biodiesel in the blend. For instance, "B5" indicates a blend with 5% biodiesel and 95% diesel fuel; in consequence, B100 indicates pure biodiesel

Advantages of the Use of Biodiesel

Some of the advantages of using biodiesel as a replacement for diesel fuel are:

• Renewable fuel, obtained from vegetable oils or animal fats.

• Low toxicity, in comparison with diesel fuel.

• Degrades more rapidly than diesel fuel, minimizing the environmental consequences of biofuel spills.

• Lower emissions of contaminants: carbon monoxide, particulate matter, polycyclic aromatic hydrocarbons, aldehydes.

• Lower health risk, due to reduced emissions of carcinogenic substances.

• No sulfur dioxide (SO_2) emissions.

• Higher flash point (100_C minimum).

• May be blended with diesel fuel at any proportion; both fuels may be mixed during the fuel supply to vehicles.

• Excellent properties as a lubricant.

• It is the only alternative fuel that can be used in a conventional diesel engine, without modifications.

• Used cooking oils and fat residues from meat processing may be used as raw materials.

Disadvantages of the Use of Biodiesel

There are certain disadvantages of using biodiesel as a replacement for diesel fuel that must be taken into consideration:

• Slightly higher fuel consumption due to the lower calorific value of biodiesel.

• Slightly higher nitrous oxide (NOx) emissions than diesel fuel.

• Higher freezing point than diesel fuel. This may be inconvenient in cold climates.

• It is less stable than diesel fuel, and therefore long-term storage (more than six months) of biodiesel is not recommended.

• May degrade plastic and natural rubber gaskets and hoses when used in pure form, in which case replacement with Teflon components is recommended.

RAW MATERIALS FOR BIODIESEL PRODUCTION

The raw materials for biodiesel production are vegetable oils, animal fats and short chain alcohols. The oils most used for worldwide biodiesel production are rapeseed (mainly in the European Union countries), soybean (Argentina and the United States of America), palm (Asian and Central American countries) and sunflower, although other oils are also used, including peanut, linseed, safflower, used vegetable oils, and also animal fats. Methanol is the most frequently used alcohol although ethanol can also be used. Since cost is the main concern in biodiesel production and trading (mainly due to oil prices), the use of non-edible vegetable oils has been studied for several years with good results. Besides its lower cost, another undeniable advantage of non-edible oils for biodiesel production lies in the fact that no foodstuffs are spent to produce fuel.

These and other reasons have led to medium- and large-scale biodiesel production trials in several countries, using non-edible oils such as castor oil, tung, cotton, jojoba and jatropha. Animal fats are also an interesting option, especially in countries with plenty of livestock resources, although it is necessary to carry out preliminary treatment since they are solid; furthermore, highly acidic grease from cattle, pork, poultry, and fish can be used. Microalgae appear to be a very important alternative for future biodiesel production due to their very high oil yield; however, it must be taken into account that only some species are useful for biofuel production. Although the properties of oils and fats used as raw materials may differ, the properties of biodiesel must be the same, complying with the requirements set by international standards.

Typical Oil Crops Useful for Biodiesel Production

The main characteristics of typical oil crops that have been found useful for biodiesel production are summarized in the following paragraphs:

Rapeseed and Canola

Rapeseed adapts well to low fertility soils, but with high sulfur content. With a high oil yield (40–50%), it may be grown as a winter-cover crop, allows double cultivation and crop rotation. It is the most important raw material for biodiesel production in the European Community. However, there were technological limitations for sowing and harvesting in some Central and South American countries, mainly due to the lack of adequate information about fertilization, seed handling, and storage (the seeds are very small and require specialized agricultural machinery). Moreover, low prices in comparison to wheat (its main competitor for crop rotation) and low production per unit area have limited its use.

Soybean

It is a legume originating in East Asia. Depending on environmental conditions and genetic varieties, the plants show wide variations in height. Leading soybean producing countries are the United States, Brazil, Argentina, China, and India. Biodiesel production form soybean yields other valuable sub-products in addition to glycerin: soybean meal and pellets (used as food for livestock) and flour (which have a high content of lecithin, a protein). Grain yield varies between 2,000 and 4,000 kg/hectare. Since the seeds are very rich in protein, oil content is around 18%.

Oil Palm

Oil palm is a tropical plant that reaches a height of 20–25 m with a life cycle of about 25 years. Full production is reached 8 years after planting. Two kinds of oil are obtained from the fruit: palm oil proper, from the pulp, and palm kernel oil, from the nut of the fruit (after oil extraction, palm kernel cake is used as livestock food). Several high oil-yield varieties have been developed. Indonesia and Malaysia are the leading producers. International demand for palm oil has increased steadily during the past years, the oil being used for cooking, and as a raw material for margarine production and as an additive for butter and bakery products.

Sunflower

Sunflower "seeds" are really a fruit, the inedible wall (husk) surrounding the seed that is in the kernel. The great importance of sunflower lies in the excellent quality of the edible oil extracted from its seeds. It is highly regarded from the point of view of nutritional quality, taste and flavor. Moreover, after oil extraction, the remaining cake is used as a livestock feed. It must be noted that sunflower oil has a very low content of linoleic acid, and therefore it may be stored for long periods. Sunflower adapts well to adverse environmental conditions and does not require specialized agricultural equipment and can be used for crop rotation with soybean and corn. Oil yield of current hybrids is in the range 48–52%.

Peanut

The quality of peanut is strongly affected by weather conditions during the harvest. Peanuts are mainly used for human consumption, in the manufacture of peanut butter, and as an ingredient for confectionery and other processed foods. Peanuts of lower quality (including the rejects from the confectionery industry) are used for oil production, which has a steady demand in the international market. Peanut oil is used in blends for cooking and as a flavoring agent in the confectionery industry. The flour left over, following oil extraction, is of high quality with high protein content; in pellet form, it is used as a livestock feed.

Safflower

Safflower adapts well to dry environments. Although the grain yield per hectare is low, the oil content of the seed is high, from 30 to 40%. Therefore, it has economic potential for arid regions. Currently, safflower is used in oil and flour production and as bird feed. There are two varieties, one rich in mono-unsaturated fatty acids (oleic acid) and the other with a high percentage of polyunsaturated fatty acids (linoleic acid). Both varieties have a low content of saturated fatty acids. The oil from safflower is of high quality and low in cholesterol content. Other than being used for human consumption, it is used in the manufacture of paints and other coating compounds, lacquers and soaps.

Castor Seed

The castor oil plant grows in tropical climates, with temperatures in the range 20–30_C; it cannot endure frost. It is important to note that once the seeds start germinating, the temperature must not fall below 12_C. The plant needs a warm and humid period in its vegetative phase and a dry season for ripening and harvesting. It requires plenty of sunlight and adapts well to several varieties of soils. The total rainfall during the growth cycle must be in the range 700–1,400 mm; although it is resistant to drought, the castor oil plant needs at least 5 months of rain during the year.

Tung

Tung is a tree that adapts well to tropical and sub-tropical climates. The optimum temperature for tung is between 18 and 26_C, with low yearly rainfall. During the harvest season, the dry nuts fall off from the tung tree and are collected from the ground. Nut production starts 3 years after the planting. The oil from tung nuts is non-edible and used in the manufacture of paints and varnishes, especially for marine use.

Cotton

Among non-foodstuffs, cotton is the most widely traded commodity. It is produced in more than 80 countries and distributed worldwide. After the harvest, it may be traded as raw cotton, fiber or seeds. In cotton mills, fiber and seeds are separated from raw cotton. Cotton fiber is processed to produce fabric and thread, for use in the textile industry.

Jojoba

Although jojoba can survive extreme drought, it requires irrigation to achieve an economically viable yield. Jojoba needs a warm climate, but a cold spell is necessary for the flowers to mature. Rainfall must be very low during the harvest season (summer). The plant reaches its full productivity 10 years after planting. The oil from jojoba is mainly used in the cosmetics industry; therefore, its market is quickly saturated.

Jatropha

Jatropha is a shrub that adapts well to arid environments. Jatropha curcas is the most known variety; it requires little water or additional care; therefore, it is adequate for warm regions with little fertility. Productivity may be reduced by irregular rainfall or strong winds during the flowering season.

Microalgae

Microalgae have great potential for biodiesel production, since the oil yield (in liters per hectare) could be one to two orders of magnitude higher than that of other raw materials. Oil content is usually from 20 to 50%, although in some species it can be higher than 70% However, it is important to note that not all microalgae are adequate for biodiesel production.

High levels of CO_2, water, light, nutrients and mineral salts are necessary for the growth of microalgae. Production processes take place in raceway ponds and photobiological reactors .

NAHAR (MESSUA FERREA)

For the current project we have selected *Mesua ferrea*(Nahar) as a source of raw material. *Mesua ferrea*(Nahar) is a species in the familyCalophyllaceae. The tree can grow over 30 m (98 ft) tall, often buttressed at the base with a trunk up to 2 m (6 ft 7 in) in diameter. The bark of younger trees has an ash grey color with flaky peelings, while of old trees the bark is dark ash-grey with a red-brown blaze. The fruit is an ovoid to globose capsule with one to two seeds.In India, it is abundant in North east region, Uttar Pradesh and Western Ghat. Biodiesel from Mesua ferrea seeds has immense scope in NE Region of India. It is estimated that more than a 10 million Kg of Nahar seeds are produced annually in the State of Assam. Nahar trees can be planted on the wasteland, roadside and in the forests. The use of non-edible vegetable oils is significant in developing countries. Edible oils have great demand as food and thus they are too expensive to be used as a fuel.

Mesua ferrea is one of the non-edible plants and a source of straight vegetable oil (SVO). Investigations have been carried out to determine various physical and chemical properties of SVO of mesua ferrea. Results have shown that these SVOs have high viscosity, high density, and low volatility as compared to diesel. The properties of SVOs were found to improve by dilution and transesterification. The effects of dilution of SVO with diesel have been studied,and it has been found that 15% SVO can be used in CI engine. Mesua ferrea produces high-oil content seeds (58–75%). Its oil contains both saturated and unsaturated fatty acids and triglycerides of linoleic, oleic, palmitic, and stearic acids. It was also found that its oil contained essentially 74.6% unsaturated fatty acids comprising mainly of oleic acid (52.3%) and linoleic acid (22.3%) and 25.4% saturated fatty acids.It is estimated that more than 10 million kilogram of mesua ferrea seeds are produced annually in the Assam. Not all these seeds find utilization in production of biodiesel.

TRANSESTERIFICATION REACTION

Vegetable oils are chemically complex esters of fatty acids. These are the fats naturally present in oil seeds, and known as tri-glycerides of fatty acids. The general method to produce biodiesel is transesterification of non-edible oil with methanol in the presence of either base or strong acid catalysts. It is the chemical conversion of oil to its corresponding fatty ester in the presence of a catalyst. Transesterification process helps reduce the viscosity of the oil. The formation of fatty acid methyl esters (FAME) through transesterification of seed oils requires raw oil, 15% of methanol & 5% of sodium hydroxide on mass basis. Methanol and ethanol are used most frequently; especially methanol is preferred because of its low cost and its physical and chemical advantages.

Transesterification of natural glycerides with methanol to methylesters is a technically important reaction that has been used extensively in the soap and detergent manufacturing industry worldwide for many years. Almost all biodiesel is produced in a similar chemical process using base catalyzed transesterification as it is the most economical process, requiring only low temperatures and pressures while producing a 98% conversion yield. The transesterification process is the reaction of a triglyceride (fat/oil) with an alcohol to form esters and glycerol. A triglyceride has a glycerine molecule as its base with three long chain fatty acids attached. The characteristics of the fat are determined by the nature of the fatty acids attached to the glycerine. The nature of the fatty acids can, in turn, affect the characteristics of the biodiesel.

During the esterification process, the triglyceride is reacted with alcohol in the presence of a catalyst, usually a strong alkaline like sodium hydroxide. The alcohol reacts with the fatty acids to form the mono-alkyl ester, or biodiesel, and crude glycerol. In most production, methanol or ethanol is the alcohol used (methanol produces methyl esters, ethanol produces ethyl esters) and is base catalyzed by either potassium or sodium hydroxide. Potassium hydroxide has been found more suitable for the ethyl ester biodiesel production, but either base can be used for methyl ester production.

The figure below shows the chemical process for methyl ester biodiesel. The reaction between the fat or oil and the alcohol is a reversible reaction, so the alcohol must be added in excess to drive the reaction towards the right and ensure complete conversion.

The products of the reaction are the biodiesel itself and glycerol.

A successful transesterification reaction is signified by the separation of the methyl ester (biodiesel) and glycerol layers after the reaction time. The heavier co-product, glycerol, settles out and may be sold as is or purified for use in other industries, e.g. pharmaceutical, cosmetics, and detergents.

After the transesterification reaction and the separation of the crude heavy glycerin phase, the producer is left with a crude light biodiesel phase. This crude biodiesel requires some purification prior to use.

Acid-Catalyzed Processes

The transesterification process is catalyzed acids, preferably by sulfonic and sulfuric acids. These catalysts give very high yields in alkyl esters, but the reactions are slow, requiring, tipically, temperatures above 100 °C and more than 3 h to reach complete conversion. Pryde *et al.* showed that the methanolysis of soybean oil, in the presence of 1 mol% of H_2SO_4, with an alcohol/oil molar ratio of 30:1 at 65 °C, takes 50 h to reach complete conversion of the vegetable oil (> 99%), while the butanolysis (at 117 °C) and ethanolysis (at 78 °C), using the same quantities of catalyst and alcohol, take 3 and 18 h, respectively.

The alcohol/vegetable oil molar ratio is one of the main factors that influences the transesterification. An excess of the alcohol favors the formation of the products. On the other hand, an excessive amount of alcohol makes the recovery of the glycerol difficult, so that the ideal alcohol/oil ratio has to be established empirically, considering each individual process.

According to this mechanism, carboxylic acids can be formed by reaction of the carbocation II with water present in the reaction mixture. This suggests that an acid-catalyzed transesterification should be carried out in the absence of water, in order to avoid the competitive formation of carboxylic acids which reduce the yields of alkyl esters.

Base-Catalyzed Processes

The base-catalyzed transesterification of vegetable oils proceeds faster than the acid-catalyzed reaction. Due to this reason, together with the fact that the alkaline catalysts are less corrosives than acidic compounds, industrial processes usually favor base catalysts, such as alkaline metal alkoxides and hydroxidesas well as sodium or potassium carbonates.

The mechanism of the base-catalyzed transesterification of vegetable oils is shown in Scheme 6. The first step (Eq. 1) is the reaction of the base with the alcohol, producing an alkoxide and the protonated catalyst. The nucleophilic attack of the alkoxide at the carbonyl group of the triglyceride generates a tetrahedral intermediate from which the alkyl ester and the corresponding anion of the diglyceride are formed The latter deprotonates the catalyst, thus regenerating the active species which is now able to react with a second molecule of the alcohol, starting another catalytic cycle. Diglycerides and monoglycerides are converted by the same mechanism to a mixture of alkyl esters and glycerol.

FUEL CHARACTERISTICS

VISCOSITY

Viscosity is the property of a fluid by virtue of which it offers resistance to flow. The viscosity of a biodiesel is higher than the viscosity of fossil-diesel and some researchers have reported that the biodiesel viscosity can be up to 1.6 times that of diesel at 40 °C . This ratio increases especially when the temperature is below 25 °C . Blending of the biodiesel with diesel and pre-heating of the biodiesel improves the viscous characteristics significantly.

DENSITY

Density is a key fuel property, which directly affects the engine performance characteristics. Many performance characteristics, such as cetane number and heating value, are related to the density . On the other hand, diesel fuel injection systems measure the fuel by volume. So the changes in the fuel density will influence engine output power due to a different mass of fuel injected . The density and viscosity of the fuels affect the start of injection, the injection pressure, and the fuel spray characteristic, so that they influence the engine performance, combustion and exhaust emissions.

CETANE NUMBER

Similar to the octane number rating that is applied to gasoline to rate its ignition stability, cetane number is the rating assigned to diesel fuel to rate its combustion quality.

While gasoline's <u>octane number</u> signifies its ability to resist auto-ignition (also referred to as pre-ignition, knocking, pinging, or detonation), diesel's cetane number is a measure of the fuel's delay of ignition time (the amount of time between the injection of fuel into the combustion chamber and the actual start of combustion of the fuel charge).

CETANE NUMBERS OF VARIOUS DIESEL FUELS

Normal modern highway diesels run best with a fuel rated between 45 and 55. Following is a list of cetane numbers varying grades and types of compression ignition diesel fuels:

Regular diesel--48

Premium diesel--55

Biodiesel (B100)--55

Biodiesel blend (B20)--50

CLOUD POINT

Cloud Point is the temperature at which the crystals of solid biodiesel first become visible. As the biodiesel starts to freeze, it will form small crystals that start clumping together. They will become visible as cloudy biodiesel when they grow to four times larger than the wavelength of visible light. At this size the crystals will easily pass through filters and can be pumped and used with no problems. As the biodiesel gets colder, the crystals get bigger and will eventually plug filters.

POUR POINT

Pour Point is the temperature where biodiesel becomes solid and can no longer be pumped. That temperature is a good bit colder than the cold filter plugging point

CALORIFIC VALUE

Calorific Value of a fuel may be defined as the amount of heat produced on complete burning of 1 kg of fuel. S.I. unit of calorific value of fuels is kilojoule per gram (KJ/kg).

FLASH POINT

Flash Point of a <u>volatile</u> material is the lowest <u>temperature</u> at which vapours of the material will ignite, when given an ignition source. The flash point is a descriptive characteristic that is used to distinguish between <u>flammable</u> liquids, such as <u>petrol</u>, and <u>combustible</u> liquids, such as <u>diesel</u>.

It is also used to characterize the <u>fire hazards</u> of liquids. Depending on the standard used, liquids which have a flash point less than either 37.8 or 60.5 °C (100.0 or 140.9 °F) are called flammable — whereas liquids having a flash point above that temperature are called combustible.

CHAPTER TWO

LITERATURE REVIEW

Non Edible Sources of Oil

Balat M. and Balat H. (2011), have said that karanja is a medium-sized green tree from the *legumnosae* family. It grows approximately 15–25 m in height. Flowering starts three to four years after plantation, and it matures four to seven years after. Recently, karanja has been recognized as an invaluable source of oil. A single tree is said to yield 9–90 kg of seeds. Several researchers have discovered the large variability of oil content in karanja seed oil. The seed contains approximately 25–40 wt. % oil.

Pinzi S. *et al.* (2009), said that Karanja mainly grows in Southeast Asia and has been successfully introduced in humid tropical regions of the world and part of China, the United States, and Australia.

Azam M. *et al.* (2005), said that Polanga is a large- or medium-sized green tree that grows in deep soil or on exposed sea sand. It belongs to the *Clusiaceae* family. The rainfall requirement of polanga seed plantation is 750 mm/ year to 5000 mm/year. The tree has multiple origins, such as Southeast Asia, India, East Africa, and Australia.

Sahoo P. *et al.* (2007), said that Its growth rate is 1 m in height, and it yields approximately 100 fruits/kg to 200 fruits/kg. Oil yield per unit area is approximately 2000 kg/ha (cite). The seed has a high oil content of 65–75 wt. %. The oil is thick and nutty smelling.

Balat M. and Balat H. (2010), have said that Mahua is a large-sized evergreen or semi-evergreen tree from the *Sapotaceae* family. Mahua is a forest-based tree largely produced in India It is cultivated in warm and humid regions for its oleaginous seeds (producing 20–200 kg of seeds annually per tree, depending on maturity), flowers, and wood. Mahua oil fat (solid at ambient temperature) has been used in skin care and in manufacturing soap or detergents. The mahua tree starts producing seeds 10 years after plantation and continues to do so up to 60 years. Tree growth is approximately 20 m in height, and its seed has an oil content of 35–50 wt. %.

Ahmad J. *et al.* (2014), has said that Rubber seed oil comes from the *Euphorbiaceae* family. This tree originates from Brazil. It is a forest-based tree largely produced in Malaysia, India, Thailand, and Indonesia. In the wild, plant height can reach up to 34 m. The tree requires heavy rainfall and non-frost climate condition. Rubber seed contains 50–60 wt. % oil, and its kernel contains 40–50 wt. % of brown oil

Fontaras G. *et al.*(2012), found that Cotton seed oil is extracted from the seeds of the cotton plant of various species, mainly *Gossypium hirsutum* and *Gossypium herbaceum*, which are grown for cotton fiber. Cotton plant grows mainly in China, the United States, and Europe. Crude cotton seed oil contains several types of non-glyceride materials, such as gossypol, phospholipids, sterols, resins, carbohydrates, and related pigments. Cotton seed oil has a density that ranges from 0.917 g/cm3 to 0.933 g/cm3. The seed contains 17–25 wt. % oil.

Huzayyin A. *et al.* (2004), said that Jojoba is native to the Mojave and Sonoran deserts of California, Arizona, and Mexico. The jojoba tree is from the *Simmondsiaceae* family. Jojoba has been grown commercially for its oil, a liquid wax ester, extracted from the seed. The plant has been used to combat and prevent desertification in some parts of India. The jojoba tree grows to a height of 1–2 m, and it has a broad and dense crown. The leaves are oval in shape, approximately 2–4 cm long and 1.5–3 cm broad; they are thick, waxy glaucous grayish green.

Kumar A. and Sharma S. (2011), have said that Neem is a medium-sized evergreen tree from the *Meliaceae* family. The tree grows 12–18 m in height. The neem tree can grow in all kinds of soil, including saline, clay, dry, shallow, alkaline, and stony soils, and even in highly calcareous soil. Neem grows in several Asian countries, such as Sri Lanka, Pakistan, India, Bangladesh, Japan, Malaysia, Indonesia, and Burma, and in the tropical regions of Australia. Normally, neem thrives in areas with sub-arid to subhumid conditions and with an annual rainfall of 400–1200 mm. It reaches a maximum productivity of 15 years after plantation, with a life span of approximately 150–200 years. Neem seed contains 20–30 wt. % oil, and its kernels contain 40–50% brown oil

Puhan S. *et al.* (2009), has said Linseed is an herbaceous annual-type plant that grows in countries such as India, Canada, Argentina, and some parts of Europe. Linseed contains 35–45 wt. %.

Kibazohi O. and Sangwan R.S. (2011), have said that Jatropha is a small tree from the *Euphorbiaceae* family, and it grows 5–7 m in height Jatropha thrives in arid, semi-arid, and tropical areas with an annual rainfall of 1000–1500 mm. The jatropha plant is native to the United States, Brazil, Bolivia, Argentina, Mexico, Africa, Paraguay, and India.

2.2 Edible Sources Of Oil

Liaquat A.M. *et al.* (2015), studied the effect of coconut biodiesel blended fuels on engine performance and emission characteristics and found that there is a decrease in torque and brake power, while increase in specific fuel consumption has been observed for coconut biodiesel blended fuels over the entire speed range compared to net diesel fuel. In case of engine exhaust gas emissions, lower HC, CO and, higher CO_2 and NO_x emissions have been found for coconut biodiesel blended fuels compared to diesel fuel. Finally, it was concluded that CB5 and CB15 can be used in diesel engines without any engine modifications.

Abu-Hamdeh H.*et al.* (2015), did a study of almond oil as a bio-diesel for diesel engine in terms of emissions and performance. It was found that almond biodiesel resulted in improved performance over the load range considered as indicated by lower brake specific fuel consumption, higher thermal efficiency, and higher exhaust gas temperature. In terms of emissions, almond biodiesel resulted in lower carbon monoxide (CO), oxides of nitrogen (NO_x), total particulate and unburned fuel emissions in the exhaust gas.

Nagi J. *et al.* (2008),researched the use ofpalm biodiesel as an alternative green renewable energy for the energy demands of the future. It has been found that palm biodiesel meets the combustion requirements of diesel engine combustion with some advantages such as low fuel consumption, less concentration of exhaust gas emission, higher combustion pressure and longer combustion period. However, it produces marginally low performance in terms of torque, thermal efficiency and higher NOx emissions as compared to petroleum diesel.

2.3 Literature Review on Biodiesel

Saxena P. *et al.* (2011),emphasized on Biodiesel as a potential and sustainable substitute for petrol and diesel. Due to the dearth of experimental data for the various thermodynamic properties of feed oils and other important properties of Biodiesel, there is a need to develop accurate model for the prediction of various properties of Biodiesel and its Blends.

Ali H. *et al.* (2013), studied the aspects related to the production of biodiesel from Neem oil. Neem oil has potential as an alternative energy source. But it is not possible for oil alone to solve dependency on foreign oil within any particular time frame. The organized plantation and systematic collection of Neem oil, being potential bio-diesel substitutes will reduce the import burden of crude petroleum.

Sathiyagnanam A.P. *et al.* (2016), studied methyl ester of mango seed and they concluded that the diesel engine can perform satisfactorily on methyl ester of mango seed oil and its blends with diesel fuel.

Sharma M. *et al.* (2007), have studied blends of Jatropha and Palm biodiesel and concluded that Jatropha biodiesel, when blended with palm methyl ester leads to a composition having efficient and improved low temperature property as well as good oxidation stability.

Mohsin R. *et al.*(2014), studied the engine performance and exhaust emission of dual fuel engine; fuelled by diesel, biodiesel, diesel–CNG, and biodiesel–CNG. The results obtained indicate that pollutant emissions such as CO and NOx emissions can be reduced by having clean combustion in the engine. Meanwhile, in term of engine power, it was observed that the combination of biodiesel and CNG increased the reading with the increase of engine speed.

Vallinayagam R. (2014), attempted to use double biofuel, pine oil–KME blends, in a diesel engine and thereby, exclude the use of fossil diesel completely. The properties of the resultant blends are found to be mutually agreeable and conducive for operation in a diesel engine.

Monirul I.M. *et al.* (2015), conducted experiments on palm oil. Results shows that the average brake power for PB10 and PB20 were 9.31% and 12.93% lower respectively compared with that for diesel fuel. PB20 is suitable for use in diesel engines without the need for any engine modification. Average CO and HC emissions of palm biodiesel blends were reduced more than diesel.

Devan P.K. *et al.* (2009), studied the performance, emission and combustion characteristics of a DI diesel engine using poon oil-based fuels. Poon oil are tested as diesel fuels in Neat and blended forms.An increase of 2.13% in brake thermal efficiency was obtained for MEPO 40 blend.There was an increase in smoke emissions for Neat poon oil and Neat 20 by 10% and 8% respectively at full load.

Baruah K. *et al.* (1984), developed a process of conversion of mesua ferrea seed oil to petroleum-like crude oil. The oil extracted from the seeds was found to be similar to mineral crude oil. Laboratory experiments have shown that the crude oil extracted from mesua ferrea seed can easily be blended with mineral crude oil.

Kushwah Y.S. *et al.* **(2008),**studied Fuel Characteristics of Mesua Ferrea and found that High viscosity is one of the main drawbacks of mesua ferrea oil. Viscosity can be reduced by transesterification process, micro-emulsion, and dilution by blending of vegetable oil with Diesel

Kushwah Y.S. *et al.* **(2008),**found that he dilution of mesua ferrea oil with petrodiesel results in homogeneous mixture for all levels of mixing. The mesua ferrea oil was mixed in proportions of 5%, 15%, 30%, and 50%. They found that 15% mesua ferrea has a viscosity and density very close to that of diesel. So, They concluded that 15% blend can be used to run the stationary CI engine.

Papu N.H. *et al.* **(2015),** studied the Performance and Emission Characteristics of a Diesel Engine run by Blend of Nahar oil methyl ester(NOME) and Waste Cooking Oil Methyl Ester(WCME) and found that Fuel consumption of NOME blend is 0.38KG/KWH at 4KW BP which is highest. N20WC80 and WCME blend was found to be lowest compared to other biodiesel blends at 4 kW BP.Also, the Exhaust Gas Temperature (EGT) of WCME blend was highest followed by N20WC80 blend which may be due to the oxygen content of the WCME, which improves combustion and thus may increase the exhaust gas temperature and EGT of other biodiesel blends were similar with neat diesel. It was observed that 60 to 80 percentage of WCME blend with NOME is the optimum blend that gives good fuel properties, engine performance and reduced smoke emission.

Tatik O.*et al.* **(2015),** studied thePerformance and Emission Characteristics of A Diesel Engine Run by Blend of Nahar and Jatropha Methyl Ester. And found that the Brake thermal efficiency found to be highest for JOME blend which is 25% at 4KW BP followed by N20J80 blend which is 24.2% at 4KW BP. The NOX emission increase as JOME vol% blend in NOME increases, this may be associated with the oxygen content of the JOME. It was concluded that 60 percentage of JOME blend with NOME is the optimum blend that gives good fuel properties, engine performance and reduced smoke emission.

Basumatary S.(2012), studied the Non-Edible Oils of Assam as Potential Feedstocks for Biodiesel Production and found that in the forests of North East India particularly in Assam, a large variety of non-edible oilseed bearing trees and shrub species are available for use as a biodiesel.

Considering oil content, abundant availability and other fuel properties of the biodiesel that meet the properties prescribed in the biodiesel standards ASTM D6751 and EN 14214,the four species available in Assam (NE region of India) areyellow oleander (*Thevetia peruviana*), koroch (*Pongamia glabra*), terminalia (*Terminalia belerica*) and nahar (*Mesua ferrea*).This species will be a sustainable resource replacing petroleum-derived diesel oil without significantly affecting the global food economy.

Dutta N. *et al.* (2007), investigated the structural analysis and rheological behavior of unheated & heated mesua ferrea seed oil reveals that there is structural variation during heat treatment at different temperatures. The structural properties like acid value, iodine value, saponification value and specific gravity value for heated oil is more then the unheated oil as shown in Table No.3. As far as the rheological behavior is concerned the co-relation is established between variation of viscosity and time of heating of the heated oil. There is slower rate of rising viscosity in the initial stage of heating this may be due to the inhibition action of natural antioxidants such as mesuol, an aromatic phenolic type compound present in the Nahar seed oil.

Summary of extensive literature survey

An exhaustive literature review is carried out on alternative fuel, raw material for biodiesel, fuel characteristics and nahar oil. Based on the literature review, it is aimed to prepare the biodiesel from nahar seeds and study its fuel characteristics.

To fulfil the aim of the project the following objectives were made.

1. Collect Nahar seeds and get nahar oil ready.
2. Prepare biodiesel by transesterification process.
3. Study the fuel characteristics of the crude as well as prepared biodiesel.

CHAPTER THREE

EXPERIMENTAL SETUP AND PROCEDURE

EQUIPMENTS USED
1. Density meter
2. Kinematic viscometer
3. Flash point tester
4. Bomb calorimeter
5. Pour point and cloud point apparatus

PROPERTY DETERMINATION

Density

The density of fuel is measured by density/specific gravity meter. Firstly the temperature of density meter is set to 15 deg. Celsius left out until it gets stabilised. The density meter has been calibrated with dry air and pure water. After some time the bio diesel has been sampled by sampling pump and reading were taken down.

Kinematic viscosity

Kinematic viscosity of the fuel is measured by kinematic viscometer bath (220/440V, single/Three phase).

Flash Point

Flash point of the fuel is determined through Flash point Tester. The flash point test is carried out by exposing a biodiesel sample, in a closed cup, to a flame at temperature controlled warming until the steam generated burns and is detected by a quick flash. A sample of diesel is suitable for use when the flash point value is above 38 °C.

Pour Point and Cloud point

Pour and cloud point of the biodiesel is examined by using pour and cloud point Apparatus. Cloud point and pour point are indicators of the lowest temperature of utility for petroleum products. The sample of biodiesel has been put inside the apparatus and sample is periodically examined while it is being cooled in the cloud and pour point apparatus. The highest temperature at which haziness is observed (cloud point), or the lowest temperature at which movement of the oil is observed (pour point), is reported as the test result.

Calorific value

Calorific value of Biodiesel has been successfully found out by using an apparatus called Bomb calorimeter.

EXPERIMENTAL PROCEDURE:

Collection of Seeds

Nahar seeds were collected from forests of Arunachal Pradesh and Assam.

Moisture Removal of the Seeds

The seeds were dried out in the Sun for 3-4 days to remove the moisture from the seeds.

Extraction of Oil

The oil was extracted from the seeds using Mahindra 6 Volt Mechanical Oil Expeller.

Filtration of Oil

The extracted oil contents many impurities in the form of sediments, this sediments present in the oil were removed using filter paper.

Transesterification of Nahar Oil

60 ml Nahar oil was poured in a round bottom flask and mixed with 360 ml Methanol in the ratio 1:6. A solution containing 0.1N HCL was poured into round bottom flask containing the oil alcohol mixture while stirring the mixture continuously.The mixture was then heated in a heating mantle at 80 deg Celsius for 4h and then allowed to settle under gravity in a separating funnel. Out of two layers formed, upper layer was of Nahar oil methyl ester (NOME) and lower layer was of glycerol. The lower was separated out and ester was mixed with hexane in the same amount and shaken properly and again allowed to settle down for 24h. The remaining mixture from the purified ester was removed. Then the hexane was allowed to vaporise in the atmosphere by keeping the mixture open for 48 hours. The ester was then blended with diesel oil in various concentrations for preparing biodiesel blends, which were subsequently used in the characterization tests. The level of blending for convenience is referred as BXX. The XX indicates the amounts of biodiesel in percentage in the blend (a B20 blend is 20% biodiesel and 80% diesel oil).

CHAPTER FOUR

RESULTS AND DISCUSSION

4.1 Oil content of Nahar seeds.

We have obtained 11.5 litres of nahar oil from 21kgs of nahar seeds, so the oil content in nahar seed was found 54.76% which is higher than many sources of non edible seeds.

4.2 Effect of Transesterification.

The properties of nahar oil was found to be highly deviating from diesel fuel, which makes it inappropriate to be used in diesel engine, but after transesterification reaction of nahar oil its properties becomes a bit close to that of diesel oil.

4.3 Effect of Blending.

Blending of Nahar oil methyl ester with diesel fuel shows properties very close to that of diesel fuel, It was observed that density and kinematic viscosity of Nahar oil methyl ester reduced while the calorific value increases when NOME is mixed with diesel.

4.4 Comparison of properties of Nahar seed oil and FAME with otheroils and FAMEs

Properties of Nahar seed oil and its FAME are observed with properties of the other tree seed based biodiesels. Density of Nahar seed oil was found to be 952 kg/m^3 which was higher than the density of Jatropha and Karanja. The density of the oil however reduced to 912.93 kg/m^3 after transesterification and thus falls within the acceptable range of 860–920 kg/m^3.

4.5 Comparison of properties of various blends.

The results shows that density, kinematic viscosity, flash point, cloud point and pour point increases with the increase in blend percentage but with increase in blend percentage the calorific value decreases.

It was also observed that Density, Kinematic Viscosity, Flash Point, Pour Point and Cloud Point increases with increase in blend % , whereas Calorific

Value decreases with increase in blend%.

SUMMARY

Based on the exhaustive fuel characterization done on the crude Nahar oil as well as on transeterified NOME, the following conclusions can be drawn:

- Nahar oil has immense scope as an alternate fuel to diesel in India. NOME has got calorific value 35.63 MJ/m3 which is quite good.
- With blending it is found that calorific value increased from 35.63 MJ/kg for NOME B100 to 37.58 MJ/kg For NOME B50.
- Although flash point of NOME B100 and B50 is higher than petroleum diesel, it is observed that with blending flash point reduces.
- Cloud point and pour point of petroleum diesel is found to be almost similar to NOME 50.

Hence, it observed that Nahar oil has got very good potentiality for using in CI engine as alternate fuel. It is also seen that with transesterification and blending the fuel properties enhances.

FUTURE SCOPE

In the present work, only the characterization of the fuel is shown to be done. In future, engine performance of nahar oil methyl ester and its blends may be tested to check whether this fuel will be feasible or not in a compression ignition engine.